PROFEXXION
Volume 1

XAVIER G. POULSON

Copyright © 2020 Xavier G. Poulson
All rights reserved.
ISBN: 9798612817468
Independently Published

We must build heaven to become immortal.

TO LOVE A WHORE

The meaning of my life
Is different to yours
My heart is broken
Mind full of flaws.

I fed you my pain
Regret the choices I made
Like a wounded bird
I am best left unsaved.

Neglected and hopeless
Calling for the one
Nobody warned me
That love makes you numb.

Ordinary frown yet
A one of a kind smile
Let me lie down
I deserve peace through exile.

The repressed struggles
Sounds of tormented screams
I promise that all
Is not as it seems.

Trips through the desert
Such a pleasant feeling
Tainted by dishonesty
A lack of healing.

The time has come
For me to find tranquillity
To keep on smiling
Own some responsibility.

The truth is too painful
Impossible to swallow
My life isn't worth living
If I feel this hollow.

So before I go to sleep
And leave my bridges to burn
Tell me honestly…

Were you my girl,
Or just my turn?

UNFIXABLE

Despite how the bitterness evolved
we never stopped laughing,
was this a sign
that it could be resolved?

No
You cannot love someone who hates your flaws.

    There's still time…

SOUL ACHE

My soul is aching
There's no use in faking
For the family see's through my lies,
Remind them of what I really love.

Shot in the heart with great precision
Relax my mind as I make the incision
For the devil knows of my actions,
Remind him of what I really hate.

I swallow my pride and put on a brave face
Keep the knife close and leave no trace
For the lord takes what I loved the most,
Remind him of what I really believe.

Pause time so I can breathe
Lock the doors so she can't leave
For the people demand what I crave the least,
Remind them of what I really feel.

My soul is aching
I can feel your body shaking
For I only know the truth,
Remind me of what I did wrong?

IGNORANCE CAKE

Tired of being alone in my head,
I need a slice
of ignorance cake
to settle the mind
but my vision keeps flashing
images of the bloodiest war
fought by the entitled
lost by the realists
forever engraved
into the tombstones
of the idealists.

JIGSAW PUZZLE

I pick up the pieces of my broken heart
Depressed so long
I forgot how to laugh
Put myself back together
What have I found?

A shell of my former self
Strong yet fragile
Free but bound.

    I'm still missing a piece…

THE ALPINE LODGE

This emotion inside
It chills me to the core
A wind so blistering
Could wash away the pain
As I'm knocked to the floor
Ivory falls from my pocket
An illness so chronic
Torture myself with the truth
As treat myself to time
Where I prey upon the public.

Now I'm lost in an urban mess
Questioning if I was ever sane
Long lost searching
For a hidden place
Where I can hide my distress
Asking the voices
Inside my head
If I can feel the same?

THE MAN WHO NO LONGER NEEDS A MASK

Growing up
nobody knew the real me,
my former personality
is now a ghost of a depressing past
that plagues my thoughts
during sleepless dreams
of a dystopian reality
I know will never last,
analyse the features
of my false face
notice the anger
the frustration
the hate
embrace the brutality
and match my pace
know you can't win this race
so back away
start running fast,
I am the man who no longer needs a mask.

LOVE RUSH

So hard to break through
my memory is cloudy
you don't know how special you are,
afraid I have lost you
the pictures that we drew
resemble the damage to
my knackered heart,
indisposed thoughts
a chance at redemption
wish we could restart
but it was over
before it began,
that's what happens when
you move too fast.

TREE HUGGERS

I should have let you go
Despite all your pleas
We were far too young
To be hugging trees,
Now I feel your pain
Alone in my constraint
Recalling what you said
You're still inside my head.

You try to take what's mine
And put all the blame on me
Knowing what we have done
It's taking control of me,
Forever lost through space
In time we'll see
The truth about
You and me.

I have to let you go
You're too hard to please
We were far too young
To be hugging trees,
Now I feel the same
Afraid I'll go insane
Despite what you've said
I want you out my head.

MONDAY NIGHT

Monday night
I'm feeling right
Between your legs
I take a chance
Drowning me
In moments
Unforgivable
You tell me
It's not the time
To take a glance
But what I thought
Would never last
Has proved me wrong
Afraid to grasp
At what is mine
I take my clothes
Run out the door
These warning signs
I can't ignore
Remind me of
Our verbal fight
On that lonesome
Monday night.

LISTEN TO YOUR OTHER HALF

Slippery words
makes for the best propaganda,
let them consume your psyche
as you purge your heart
and let their advice
cut down your terrors,
for you are so alike.

TAKE IT TO THE GRAVE

Lambasted by his words
Sickening and stupid
He deserves to be hurt
Presuming his fate
Will be the same as mine
We miserably failed
There's no one to blame
Stale and frigid
Only God will know
Of his horrific crime.

CAT MAN

I am a cat man
Despite my love for dogs
I hate it when they bark
Why can't it just be stopped?

A dog will blindly follow
But a cat will choose its friends
How to make them like you
It really just depends
On how you will approach them
Startle and despair
To find a dog that's fussy
Is beyond the realms of rare.

Yes, I am a cat man
Despite my love for dogs
One thing is for certain
They're both better than a frog.

THE FIGHT FOR FREEDOM

Learn of the horror
How they stood on their knees
The history we're taught
Is morphed only to please
The radicals of the spectrum
Their morals are wrong
They'll soon take over
It won't be too long.

IN THE DARK CORNER

In the dark corner
Wrapped in despair
Even at his happiest
He contemplates death
Afraid to let go
Blind like a moth
Crippled by smitten
Never to be loved
He tears out his hair
Lost in his past
Changing what's written
Ready to be born
Free from his cast.

A HOMICIDE IN HELL

I'll never love anyone again,
damaged permanently
by the image of her soul
being tortured by the devil's disciples.

She has touched my heart
but my spirit is broken,
I bleed out
staining the carpet blue from red.

    I can see the silver…

THE DICTATOR

Speeding through the tunnel
Blinded by the light
Judge him by his kindness
Underestimate his might.

Falling through the skyline
Afraid to hit the ground
Butchered dreams of solace
His lies are so profound.

Cast away the lustful
Jinxed by the cruel
Provoke a genuine leader
Use violence as a tool.

Scrounging off the stricken
Deprived yet unbound
Nestled in warzone
A crazed toxic hound.

The apocalypse is lurking
Overthrow the tyrant's rule
Judge him by his malice
Is it wrong to murder a fool?

SELF CONTROL

Pathetic and distasteful,
your kinks are fucking shameful.

Restless and shallow,
your family is fucking callow.

    I'll stop now…

THE RIGHT TIME

Tell her I won't make it through the night
Feeling like my life is huge lie
Afraid to say it to her pretty face
How will I know when it's the right time?

Cannot feel same under her rules
She's twisting words as my blood pools
Tell her about my sins when we're both alone
How will I know when it's the right time?

Flaying my skin down to the bone
Searching for a place that I can call home
All I want is for you to hold my hand
How will I know when it's the right time?

Hear my soul wailing in the clouds
Tell her that our love knows no bounds
Feeling gone before I've even left
I don't ever want to leave her…

There's no such thing as the right time.

WEIRD WORLD

So what I'm strange,
who isn't weird in this world?

What is 'normal'
but just a word?

Invented by a vengeful being
filled with unexplained
and undeserving hatred.

MANIPULATOR

The lies won't stop
I'm wondering why
you left me in the dark,
my tears freeze up as you kiss me
I'm in need of help again
but then I feel your sweet affection
drain my life away,
you whisper my name
then I'm not so sad
it's not so bad.

WHEN YOU CLOSE YOUR EYES

When you close your eyes
It's the first thing that you want see
Protesting for a change
In who's controlling what you dream.

When you close your eyes
It's the last thing that you want to see
Screaming for a chance
To get one night of peaceful sleep.

You close your eyes
It's the first thing that you see
It's not as bad as you recall
You awaken to find
The sun has set
Yet another sleepless dream.

A MALE ACTIVIST

A young man took to the streets
campaigning for a change in rule
only to discover
that the world doesn't need his privilege.

The young man was outcasted
vengeful and self-loathing,
formulating a new plan
to drag his fellow man
down in the depths
of his pessimistic thinking.

THE KEY TO HEAVEN

Believing in mortality
it's a common lie of life,
our purpose
is to scar the world
with the energy
that makes us human -
that way of living
inevitably
leads to infinity.

AIRBORNE

Tempted by pleasure
To revisit the past
Knowing she could never love me
Cuts deeper than rejection
Filling the void that she left
A space we cannot measure
You betrayed my trust
That I cannot forgive
My soul will burn with my body
Forgotten by the masses
As our love is reduced to dust
Scattered to the wind
That'll whisper our names
Together forever.

DO YOU KNOW HOW TO LOVE?

Waking up next to strangers
So disgusting yet addictive
Steal the dignity of women
Their morals are conflicted
To love someone is sacred
Don't give away your passion
Nobody is an object
Feelings you should ration
Your intimacy is priceless
Choose wisely when you share
For they will take a piece of you
Handle love with care.

A NIHILIST'S DEATH

In my bed
Heart exposed
Letting my depression flow.

May it crush
My future dreams
All is lost or so it seems.

Winter breeze
Cools the breath
Of the ghosts I thought I fled.

Touch my skin
Hold me close
Know I'll never smile again.

Crumbling
Drenched in sweat
Doing what I do best.

Piercing eyes
Stab my chest
I can't live like this anymore.

Crawling through
My own mess
Put my body to the test.

On the edge
A blissful lie
Whisper you a lullaby.

Call for me
Loud and clear
I'm afraid I cannot hear.

Trapped inside
My unkind head
Plagued by thoughts I dread.

Frozen fear
Stuck in hell
You promised not to tell.

Now I'm gone
No regrets
Make sure you don't forget.

WIFE BEATER

It's foolish to believe
that a cold-hearted man
can shed a single tear,
know that
he snatched at your feelings
as you bled from your mouth
constricted by the fear,
know that
it's time to leave
for he'll never love you
no matter what you hear.

A CONVERSATION AT THE GATE

"I have a query
for I fail to see the legitimacy of your goals,
would you be kind enough to share some insight
on what drove you down such an immoral path?"

The Lord of Suffering smiles,
sending chills down the new arrival's spine.

"My dear child
if you think you're alone in the anguish of existence
look to the stars –
there's always another victim to my merciless wrath,
take comfort in the fact that you won't be the last."

ALONE IN MY REFLECTION

My friends are all gone
but not dead,
I just can't see them.

Honestly
I feel as though I've never been able to see them
but I shouldn't care,
because I've never been able to see myself.

FORBIDDEN THOUGHTS

We would dance in the kitchen
To our favourite songs
Cuddle until sunrise
Our love wasn't wrong.

Impossible to replace her
Love scars will never fade
She'll always be my number one
A debt that can't be paid.

I will fall in love again
In a future dream
I know you still think of me
We were once a team.

    I miss you…

A SECOND CHANCE

Strange heart
She took what I cared for the most
Losing my first love
Has made me strong
But I can't forget
How it hurt
When I go back
To the start.

SHAMEFUL HONESTY

Strapped to this concept
she's pestering me
used and abused
in this state of mind
I can only hope
that the truth
will be released.

My own company
has never felt
so comforting
as I'm wondering
if this feeling
will haunt me
until my dying breath.

I'm cut open
deceitful prayers
misspoken
when asking for
a second chance
to be loved again,
then I can finally
rest in peace.

MIND MY DESPERATION

Toad licker
Ant flicker
Get out of my head
You're making me be cruel.

Brain thicker
Heart sicker
Get out of my bed
I don't need your comfort.

    This isn't me…

I'M LEARNING TO BEHAVE

When this began,
I closed my mind and prayed
to forget about the times
we struggled night and day.

Can't face the truth,
letting out those helpless cries
waking up every morning
wishing I would die.

Too insecure,
to walk this painful road alone
without embracing the facts
that I refused to know.

Losing my youth,
as sit around and waste my time
and the fault is all mine
I know I crossed the line.

But now I have a second chance
to reverse what's been done.

I'll make amends with my past
to build a future I hope will last.

And as my scars fade away
I will make it day-by-day.

Learning the truth about
the one I couldn't save –

I'm learning to behave.

THE BROKEN MALE

What am I?
just another hopeless man
paranoid -
holding the world
in his hands
depressed
without power
forming a plan
to erase what remains
of his traumatic memories.

BLACK WIDOWS' SECRETS

Don't lie
to the men who love you,
instead
be honest
it'll give them a reason
to hate themselves.

Don't tell the truth
to the women who love you,
instead
kill yourself
for if you lie to a woman
you're already dead.

DEPRESSED LOVERS

Catching feelings wasn't part of her plan
Destined to be more than a one-night stand
The most beautiful woman from another land
He'll never forget when she grabbed his hand
She fell in love with a boy posing as a man.

Spending every day in complete bliss
Naked in a single bed and sharing a kiss
Impossible to notice that something was amiss
Blinded by smitten so he did not resist
She was strangely affectionate for a misandrist.

She showed him a brighter side of the planet
Whilst hiding her skeletons deep in the closet
The truth was malevolent and stung like a hornet
Afraid to concede so he hid in a casket
It wasn't long before he awoke in her pocket.

The couple parted ways despite their connection
The boy said nothing for he feared her rejection
The girl is now a phantom without his protection
Their love for each other was a lifetime conviction
They'll remember the good times without his depression…

COUPLES THERAPY

Help me control my emotion
and I'll save your children
from the evil
that awaits them in adulthood.

Once the plan is in motion
we'll go out to sea
only to drown ourselves,
consuming the salt
as if it will preserve our spirit.

Let's mix a love potion
we only need tears and blood,
forget about their stance
for only time will tell
whether we were meant to be.

    I never liked you…

WET BREAK

Write your name
on my wall
show no remorse
it falls,
my face twists
I've had enough
nobody told me
it would be this rough,
you came here
looking for a fight
to my dismay
you were always right,
falsify
what remains
of what we built
on that rainy day.

THE OTHER SIDE

The hearts gone cold
my spirit dies
they'll miss me when I'm gone,
pretentious thoughts cloud up my judgement
no one will know the truth,
even if I owned up to my lies
they won't let me through the gates,
I beg forgiveness
but they cast me out
plagued with doubt.

The body rots
I can't be saved
I'll never forgive myself,
hearing the cries of my family
but they can't hear me shout,
even if I tried to make amends
they won't let me through the gates,
I try to break in
but they cast me out
plagued with doubt.

The mind goes blank
dreamless sleeping
I've made an immense mistake,
precious time slips through my fingers
it's out of my control,
even if I were to show remorse
they won't let me through the gates,
I ask politely
but they cast me out
plagued with doubt.

The time has come
rain's pouring down
my soul just feels in pain,
I see my mother stand beside me
she'll never see this through,
even if I were to tell the truth
they won't let me through the gates,
I fall through the ground
to my lonely cell
in the depths of hell.

    Welcome to the Other Side…

A PICTURE OF YOUNG LOVE

I draw around the body of my lover with a crayon
only to find that I'm using my blood
to colour between the lines.

    You're draining the life out of me!

THE DEVIL WEARS A SUIT

Diversity is burning,
Let's watch and rejoice
In the name of a serpent
As we call for our freedom
But how can we feel able
If we can't speak our minds?

    Sharpen your tongue.

RIG THE DECK!

Count up the votes
O' what is of this treachery!
For we are entitled
To a corrupt democracy.

LOST BOYS

The weak curl up
Cry for their mothers
Fire burns their souls
There is no escape.

Ice melts
A band of six sing for our sins
Begging for all that is evil
To be burned at the stake
But their guitar strings are broken.

I cannot believe that I have been exposed,
A kitchen knife is slicing through my skin
The leg of a precious lamb
Grabbed and snapped
The pain will satisfy the masses –
Be thankful.

    Are you not satisfied?

A NOTE FOR THOSE STILL HOLDING ON

They don't want to see you happy,
you're wasting your time
feed them your problems
disguised as art,
watch them cry
at your success.

THE CARDIOLOGIST

Taking pills to remember our past
Sipping on gin from a rusted flask
Wondering if we were ever meant to last
Lord I pray for another impossible task.

But there's no answer…
please don't leave me in the dark,
I just started mending my heart.

Sick to my stomach when I think of her
A past so intoxicating it makes my vision blur
I throw all our photos into an urn
Mourn for our love as I take that left turn.

But there's no escape…
I've been left alone in the dark,
my time has run out
I can't mend my heart.

Kill off the pain with crystals and leaves
Capital punishment for sadists and thieves
I don't care if I get blood on my sleeves
Who's going to care for her when she grieves?

But there's no use…
she'll never visit me in the dark,
I'll learn to live with a broken heart.

YOU'LL NEVER UNDERSTAND

Delusional,
he does not have the golden brain
but only the tears of a god,
on a cold winter's day
the sun ignites the torrential rain;
blinding lights
sends his mind into a spiral,
he falls to knees
clutching at his face and screaming
"is there an end to this pain?"

STAINED SHEETS

A preposterous proposition
Stained by your odium
Inflicts intolerable laughter
That shattered my life
During dreams of expedience.

    How could you be so vile?

BE AFRIAD OF THE BEAST

Remember
free your mind from poisonous voices
there's no room for bloodcurdling noises
dogs will bark if you bite first
promiscuous riots as their lungs burst
you're nothing without me
I laugh at your pain
an animal this wild is impossible to tame.

Promise
that you'll never question my demands
be vigilant when it's time to take up arms
time will ruin you as it strengthens my grip
nothing will catch you when you slip
you're hopeless without me
curb your complaints
an animal this arrogant will fly when it faints.

Grieve
when I destroy what's left of your image
caress what remains of my elegant visage
drown your children in a shallow pool
their faces will resemble that of a ghoul
you're sad without me
admit the defeat
an animal this evil doesn't deserve a treat.

STILL GROWING

My skin is shedding,
it resembles the petals
of the world's most beautiful flower.

Plant me a seed
and I'll give you a reason to smile,
for I am the one with all the power.

THE EVILS OF PLEASURE

I miss feeling free,
when I knew less -
now I know too much.

I can't live like this,
trapped in happiness
like a kid trapped in a ball pit.

THE SORE LOSER

A broken record
that nobody cares for
has lost its vote of confidence,
we crawl out from our mansions
and laugh at the stricken
ignoring the people's decision
to live a better life.

REMEMBER HER

Clouded by dreams of death
I'm feeling the same as before
but I can't control pace
of these destructive thoughts,
I grab hold of my lover
begging her to stay
for I know I'll perish
if she leaves me in my head,
her body starts to fade away
I'm afraid that I'll forget her face
my cheeks are stained with tears
as I drop to the floor
clutching at my broken heart
knowing this has gone too far –
one last glimpse of her smile
how could I have been so vile?

TRIPPING OFF ISOLATION

Smoke weed to induce my insanity
then pretend I'm sane,
I'm a good human
but a bad alien,
the inhabitants of mars wouldn't accept me
even if I offered them cookies.

    What a trip!

OUT OF THIS WORLD

The dead keep breaking through the walls of your subconscious
their monstrous behaviour only leads to one thing
a fragmented mind,
belligerent and malevolent
it can make you feel nauseous,
even though it may seem tempting
don't give in,
just nod and be gracious
because in the comfort of your mind
you need not listen to the flirtatious,
these aliens are rude and pugnacious
it's easy to hate them
instead,
cherish the time you have with them
and learn to be vivacious.

    You're destined for great things
    trust me
    it's written in stars.

FRIGHTENING FUTURE

It's midnight
On my way home
Crying my eyes out
Pick up the phone
She wants me back
I upset the tone
Forever depressed
Coated in chrome.

HATING ON YOU

We don't need friends
Just a life that's new
Counting up what's left
I'm just hating on you.

When I'm sat facing
To the wall we built
I can see myself
Smiling but crying
Because it's true
I'm just hating on you.

Bringing me peace
Dancing in the dark
Come to me
Make your mark
For what is real
Is only simple when
I'm just hating on you.

A DREAM OF REJECTION

I picture her dancing alone
then imagine myself coming to join her
but she only screams when I'm present –
she doesn't move.

    I'm sleeping alone.

I'LL MEET YOU AT THE WISHING WELL

I'll meet you at the wishing well
where the desperate pray for pleasure
as we seek redemption
for crimes we didn't commit,
toss away our hopes
as the water rises to the waist
submerged in the depths of hell
to be tortured by our heroes
and comforted by our demons.

UNITED BY GRAFFITI

Spray paint
the face of a dead man
it represents
the coldness of the world leaders,
Earth is doomed unless we take over
the revolution is coming…

A TRAGIC LESSON

On my way to heaven
everything should be fine,
I'm not taking any risks
will she take what's mine?

Heaven doesn't exist
I'm starting to feel nervous,
train of thought is clouded
am I being reckless?

I step into the flames
she doesn't strike me as a bluffer,
ask me for a favour
do I deserve to suffer?

Back in my bedroom
where I know I should've stayed,
there's no point in crying
I know the memory will fade...

    What was I thinking?

TRUST FUND BABY

Bank on his wrist
Rob him if you dare
Warrant nothing but hate
For such envious glares.

Drowning in diamonds
Cocaine in his nose
Poverty is a state of mind
Never mind your woes.

    You're such a spoilt brat!

HELL HOME

There's something creeping in the dark
afraid to confront it
I run to wake my father
to find that he isn't in bed
and that my mother is dead,
I turn around and see the monster
staring into my eyes
it stretches out a hand –

> "Everything will be alright
> if you tell me of all your lies."

Left with no escape
I accept my fate
as it takes me by the arm
dragging me into a pit of fire
to burn with all the other liars.

Screaming in agony
I awaken
a changed man
with a clean slate
only to find
that my mother wasn't dead
she's sleeping peacefully
beside the monster in her bed.

CHILDREN OF GENOCIDE

A philosophy that killed millions
drives the youth forward
in the name of equality
they oppress the side of right
failing to see the harm
caused by their warriors.

    Why are we so uneducated?

A THREATENING THOUGHT

Analyse your spirit
recognise your lies
deceive me again
and I'll betray you,
ruining your life…

    The truth cuts deeper than the sharpest blade.

TERMINALLY IN LOVE

Today I die and there's no turning back
call him a prophet
label me a maniac,
to her I'm nothing
just another number
I pray that I never wake from this slumber.

Days wasted by
as I sit in oblivion
questioning her disturbing submissions,
my brain is in pieces
thoughts are scattered
memories altered and body battered.

Today I was supposed to die
I don't know whether to laugh or cry,
my wounds are deep
they won't stop bleeding…
can I blame my lover for fleeing?

WEAK FOUNDATIONS

Snap your bones
build new ones from concrete
become the city you live in
for we're already equal
you know nothing about suffering…

NAÏVE PARENTS

Peek out the window,
children are playing in the streets
without any toys,
they only play with body parts
of the adults that have cleansed them of their innocence.

    Let's sob for their sorrows together.

A NIGHTMARE FROM THE PAST

I cannot begin to describe what I'm seeing
It's coming right from your soul
You cannot stop it from hurting me
In the moonlight
As if you could touch me
With your icy fingers
Like the breath of a disturbed nurse
Lost in a children's hospital.

    I'm literally screaming!

A CRY FOR HELP

I weep because
it's all I know how to do
and I wish I could feel different
but it's inconceivable
for I am the only one
with the silver blood in my heart.

Sometimes
I think I'm crazy
for I can't comprehend my emotions,
watch my hands and tongue
and the truth will be revealed.

THINGS I SHOULD'VE TOLD YOU

Last time we were together
Caught between the lines
Things I should've told you,
I never said goodbye.

Thought that we would meet
At a time that never came
Things I should've told you,
I'll live with all the pain.

Know that I write to you
Every single day
Things I should've told you,
But was too afraid to say.

Last time we were together
Caught between the lines
I wish that I could see you
But I can't turn back time.

THE FLAME OF SHAME

The crackling of a burning soul
stops the world from spinning
as I divorce my family
for they know of my shame
and capacity to murder
the demons in the crevasse
of my damaged heart.

HE TAUGHT ME HOW TO COOK

I am friends with the man
whom inflicts his pain upon the innocent
as he boils his enemies in a pot of water.

    I add salt and pepper.

SEXUAL CONCUSSION

The glow in her eyes
reflects his grin,
she strips off her clothes
as he basks in sin,
these passionate lovers
make the room spin.

    This is love at its purest…

PREPARING FOR EXTINCTION

I wonder how an apocalypse would happen in my lifetime…

They open the black box
The pictures are horrific
Society needs to know the truth
Our children will be the death of us
But who cares?

An apocalypse is just a frame of mind.

DROWNING IN FAKE LOVE

I was left breathless when she entered my gaze
A woman so gorgeous set my heart ablaze.

Kissing her sent me into a state of euphoria
It's true what they say about the girls from California.

Her beauty was toxic like an exotic flower
It was plucked by a tyrant feeding off false power.

Unwillingly used, her wounds were still bleeding
You can't be mad if you crash when you're speeding.

Dreaming of time travel so I can preserve my purity
A shell of my former self crying for liberty.

Bent by the devil and whipped in the streets
I cannot rest whilst this corrupted heart beats.

On the edge of the abyss, I'll wait for the shove
I know my sprit will soar high like a dove
As my body sinks
Drowning in fake love.

KILLING MELODY

An honest man
wears his heart on his sleeves,
feel his passion
as he sings for the world to hear
to the wails of babies
being thrown away
by unloving mothers.

FORBIDDEN LANGUAGE

Why can't I swear if it pleases me?
Who's to say that cursing doesn't bring us closer to heaven,
releasing a chemical in our brains
that God created by mistake -
bask in his flaws and establish the connection.

    Fuck that!

BRAINWASHED BY THE MEDIA

Brainwashed by the media
Are the youth of the today
Leading us to oblivion
We continue to be passive
Throw away our phones
Know that they are lying
Ungrateful for their lives
Blaming what we've built
For things we cannot change
Too dumb to understand
The complexities of nature
Taunted by our leaders
Brainwashed by the media.

THE URGE

I'm in a state of mind
where I want to kiss someone
and then break a window.

Instead I imagine
slitting my wrists
then stitching them back up
before I bleed out.

Damn better than an orgasm.

TO PUNISH A VICITM

Stranded in the middle of a lake
reading the words on your face
it's nothing I haven't seen before
feeling ashamed
I rock the boat
desperate for more
but then you slap me,
I'm back in reality
sinking to the bottom
bleeding from the core
eternally lost
in this train of thought.

I know I was wrong,
could you forgive me
if I changed my ways?

ROADKILL

Smashed the windshield
The wheel is gone
Irreparable damage
Know that the end is near
For I share your concern
Feeling younger
Yet wiser
Purity and innocence
That can only be compared
To a skittish rabbit
Get me off the road!

DON'T TEST ME

Go ahead
ignore my love
but you should know that
my hatred will break through anything,
you can run
I won't chase you
because you already know
I'll always be inside your head.

    I'll get my revenge one day…

DAY DREAMING OF RED

I think she hates me,
perhaps I should ask
if she would prefer me to disappear?

I approach her,
palms sweaty
and ready to show emotion
but my mind shifts.

I'm now thinking of a bunch of grapes,
squishing them with my bare hands
to make the finest wine.

    ...were we still talking?

AN OCEAN OF REGRET

Soaked in misery
drowning in open air,
my lungs expand
crackling like a broken speaker
as I shoot the final flare.

It ignites the sky
please show me your stars,
I'm looking for answers
to the forbidden question…
can we forget our past?

MONSTERS DESERVE TO BE FORGOTTEN

If I go missing
this will be my note of ransom:

Read and illustrate
what you could have done differently,
imagine that it's your fault –
then you'll be glad I'm gone.

    You killed a villain.

THE DELUSIONAL HUSBAND

Sat in his bedroom
Face stern with a frown
Blood stained on his dressing gown
He looks at his partner
And ignores what she feels
He's foolish to believe that a broken heart heals.

SOMEONE SAID

Someone said
They saw us laughing
That goes against the rules.

Someone said
We were departing
I thought it was a secret.

Someone said
They saw us fighting
Let's give them what they want.

Someone said
We were regretting
That's closer to the truth.

Someone said
Stop the rumours
It's nothing to do with you.

PEOPLE HAVE WINGS TOO

Don't break my heart
or the butterflies will surround me
and carry my body
straight to purgatory…

…it was a matter of fate.

REVENGE OF THE OUTCASTS

You fight for freedom
But not for speech
Your words are meaningless
But continue to screech
You only look stupid
With your dyed purple hair
Go back to your mum's basement
Life will always be unfair.

SINS OF NATURE

Unto that of the snake
It lies only for wealth
Whispering phrases
One can only ponder
If it'll lose all its health.

Unto that of the bird
It sings only for sex
Comforting lyrics
One can only question
If its demands will be met.

Unto that of the rat
It squeaks only for food
Frightening concepts
One can only wonder
If its manners are rude.

Unto that of the man
He's afraid of the truth
Perplexing morals
One can only request
If he can keep his youth.

QUEST FOR RELIEF

Countless thoughts
I cannot change
Reminds me of
Those wholesome days
When we were happy
But content in pain
We failed to learn
Myself to blame
Left for less
Longing for
The sacred sign
A chance for more
To protect myself
From what's divine
That's the way
I'll save what's mine.

A DRY CLEANSE

I'm going to be sober
Take control of the wheel
Drive off into the sunset
Leave my kin to drown
Flourish in the blood of Christ
Clandestine house of healing
A sea between our broken souls
Will we learn to cure ourselves?

ENCOURAGED SELF HATRED

Bury the truth
with the corpses of the rich,
no one can discover
our secret plan
to end the world
for we are cancer
and deserve nothing less.

    (These are dangerous thoughts indeed.)

STAR GAZER

It's three o'clock in the morning
The moonlight spills on my face
As I gaze up at the flickering stars
Wondering if she's doing the same
Is it wrong for me to be this sleepless?
Oh please! I need is reassurance
The severity of this heartbreak
It's testing my endurance.

I passed with flying colours
Now I'm a changed man
Love can finally reappear
All according to my plan
I may still be a star gazer
But I no longer need to wish
My hatred is depleted
Released of all my anguish.

I'M AFRAID TO LET GO

The brightest of eyes
Revel in the snow
Melt away the heart
I'm afraid to let go.

Breathe before you speak
Describe what you know
Pick away my flesh
I'm afraid to let go.

Vastness of the night
Watch our children grow
Burn away the past
I'm afraid to let go.

Creeping in my skin
Letting the hate flow
Cast away the love
I'm afraid to let go.

I'm afraid to let go
Perceptions of a lie
There's a silver lining
Between you and I.

I'm afraid to let go
Take heed of my pleas
The strain on my heart
I know what it means.

I'm afraid to let go
Attached to the past
Fear of the future
Labelled an outcast.

I'm afraid to let go
Is it wrong to cry?
There's a silver lining
I don't want to die.

CONFESSIONS OF A HEARTBREAKER

Should have been more truthful
Embraced the love you offered
You were the best companion
I've never felt so honoured
Failed you as a boyfriend
Brought shame to my name
Deserve to be alone forever
But I can't tolerate the pain
Wonder if you think of me
As you live your happy life
There's one thing I need to tell you…

    You'll know in due time.

A poem for me
Holds a sacred truth
Although it has one meaning
It may be different for you.

Thank you for reading PROFEXXION.

ACKNOWLEDGMENTS

I would like to acknowledge my beloved family for supporting me through the development of this book, and helping me see the light during the darkest of times. I love you all very much.

I would like to acknowledge my friends who have stuck by my side and helped me in establishing a sense of belonging. Without you, this book wouldn't have been possible.

Thank you all.

Printed in Great Britain
by Amazon